FORCEFUL FLIEGERS MINUS FOLLY

FLETCHER DEWOLF

FORCEFUL FLIEGERS
FLIEGERS
MINUS FOLLY

FLETCHER DEWOLF

ARPress
ILLUMINATING IDEAS
EMPOWERING VOICES

ARPress
45 Dan Road Suite 15
Canton MA 02021

Hotline: 1(888) 821-0229
Fax: 1(508) 545-7580

Ordering Information:

Quantity sales. Special discounts are available on quantity purchases by corporations, associations, and others. For details, contact the publisher at the address above.
Printed in the United States of America.

ISBN-13:   Paperback   979-8-89676-298-0
             eBook   979-8-89676-299-7

Library of Congress Control Number: 2025911682

Dedication

To the poetic spirit within us all,
to clear the paths of positivity,
with a fullness of futures whom gather no uncertainty.

'East & West my Family'

Combining the Kestrels Wing

Theories in dyeing the verse
Inside the letters and art
Bring flurries with storm and snow
Falling inside of the heart
Riming loves dreadful arrow
With feathers from the sparrow
Have fetters of metre drake
Shadowing our last mistake
Sopped in wine beneath a poisoned tree
Growing close to shore to meet the sea

Style Weighted with Matter

In the Olden days of dwindle din
When little went right and all was thin
Feathered Words did land on a silver page
And a gold lace sound spread across the stage
A crowd did draw to pass all the day
Till minds were happy with all they'd say.

Including the Spirit

On the grave of his mistress
He broke free from life
Not long in death's hand
They had discovered the knife
Near the yard's entrance
There was a Note on the Gate
That read, "No longer shall I
have to quarrel with my fate."

This Shady Life

Seen soon to stagger
When thick grows the voice
The threads of this life
Wind round the spool of their choice
When down on ye luck
A rainbow will yield
Calling the clouds to lay low
Their blue and white shield.

The Angels of Poetic Power

Tonight we will drink
From the Pierian spring
Below the moon of wisdom
We will see everything
Wars they will windle
And cease before our feet
For never has man's mind
Had more it could meet.

Flying the Verse that Fits

The moves of wisdom
Near the weeping and worn
Have shadows that call
To the sun
Clearly born
Braking the clouds that hover
This mysterious night
Fore the last of wings find land
From the fathomless flight

Their Meek Understanding

Contribute to the literature
And crawl upon each line
The fleshly school of poetry
Has taught you how to rhyme
The swords own shadow
Scares the weak
With little words they choose to speak
How bitter is thee way of pen
While Still inside these plays of men
Each poet finds his way to bend.

Our Own Emblems

Knowable notes we all understood
Whether they're evil or crowning the good
They work at the opening next to the mind
Leaving the old cross far from our kind.

It's Well Forgotten

Tones far under the porch and hall
Open their pitch and start to call
As the lightning strikes each chapter made
Until the memory forgets to fade.

Once Upon the Mat at Door

The key of the enclosure
Will let no one get out
Till the final frozen lock
Is thrown and tossed about.
Tormented with red colors
Till they're taught to change
The purpose of each ring that's worn
Appearing mighty strange.

Historically First

Inscriptions for the beings phase
On the mountains chosen to raise
Lustrous influence lines each page
While hillsides steepen pioneers rage
A benevolent will has broken free
To take thee 'cross more written waves of sea.

Anything

David Grays gone to dig some more
Searching fame and poetic war
The Cornhill scripts have sold his view
As if before no one once knew.

Before Their Withdrawn

Scorn thru all history has been clearly said
To grow the best inside a lady's head
Though warlocks know the cogent truth
That bites the best with wisdom's tooth.

Shaking Clear of Trammels

Unfinished on the easel
The tree tops muse and stare
The wise and foolish wipe
The scenery from the air,
Peasants seek the studio
For breadth of view and calm
'Til the spring is born and new
In a cloak it calls its charm.

Those Wanting Wastrels

Sense that staggers still may stand
To walk on by the closing hand
About to rule and take the knight
Down from his horse that's trained to bite.
Beyond the moment now and then
We find one man who moves the pen
He looks in darkness and has eyes
That see what never one's surmise.
Battles on the moving key
Have been fought and won at sea
Though minds that melt and break like glass
Never have questions they may ask
Until they're formed to finely be
Away from all that is history

Inside Your Lovely Eyes

When words run dry and voids appear
We fathom more what wizards fear
The stark and dark they shiver slight
As we perform this day and night
Below the skies and past their space
This poem has flown to now replace
What's thought to be and known as true
That's captured every part of you.

The Sun

Rhyming masters meet the tailor
Stitching truth into the towns
Where people smile and start to pile
The memories of old frowns.

Seven Wrinkled Brows

The time for challenge has come
And the most descriptive plays
Acted on our marble stage
Are tombstones in each comer
That will decorate the page.

The Real Age On

Doff the biblical bribe
It's come to make you pay
Twelve men did walk to have us say,
Attention to their plight
How right it must have been
Although we know the Light
Was not all inside of them
Their Lord has cursed the others
Whomever claims to be
Of the truer power
Or on top of sorcery
Now, is not to curse a sin itself?
For he on mighty high,
And who is known most often,
For the reason men did die?

Just Like Fools

In stealthy schools of criticism
Students drool and spit
The theme to every poet's dream
They can not seem to fit
They read the titled chaptered prose
And still decide that no one knows.

From Her Claws

Witch Lord will not ever know
What secret strings have been pulled
In this potioned puppet show.

Full and By

A harpoon in deep
Now part of the whale,
With shrill voices that travel
From tongues towards the ear
Leaving in the memory
No skill to appear.
They start begging a sailor
To slip on the deck
Where coins fall from the crow's nest
That flies from the wreck.
Far over twigs on the wave
Near quills in the salt
The captain is blamed
And takes all the fault.
The crew saunters off
Without any care
That their log is saved
And served to its share.

The Eye

What holds the tailor's tattered shreds
And printers broken type
As it has the apple fall
Before it's red or ripe
Then reads heroic verses
On throughout the naked night.

Politics that Suffers from Infantile Paralysis

Visions sail upon our aqueous humor
Then reproduce inside our head
Tears come from there and stare
At what the fools have said.
If talent was the purpose
For all-life to be alive
Most would have more hard a time
Continuing to survive.
Their politics has washed the minds
Throughout this lovely land
Though there are many of us
Who live our life to understand
That their reign is artificial
And with votes they promenade
Thinking they are official
And have really got it made.

The Sac Tribe

Politics and politicians
Lose their value over night
Though poets live forever
To teach us what is chiefly right.

Anticipating A World With More Energy

Whoa! What a hatred the ink has in its pen,
It's been used upon hall of all the earth's men
"Not I," said the poet
"I am a romantic lover."
"Not I," said the novelist,
"it's scribed on the cover."
"Not I," said the playwright,
"it's only been acted out."
"Then let there be not doubt,
It's me," said the bad bard,
Man has gone on for years
And drown deep in his tears
With all fears left about,
It's the coming of studious scholars
Who kill off the mellow, mild and meek
Planning to invade a world that is weak."

All Dogs Done De-Liberating Over The Day's Donations

The lasting cerebral wheels of want and space
Have starred the universe with each moon in place
Above the mountain's slope
Are shores of some who've sailed with hope
As on the hilltops of each man's wits
There ticks the time he most often quits
So supposed by those behind each door
Who'll not figure out any more.

Bloody Hands

Leaving on tramp with bundle and stick
A travelling hedge smith thinning the thick
Fighting the griffons hard bite and bark
Feeling it had found a man of no mark.

They Have No Eye Dear

For skulls that speak below their bated breath
Of graveyards custom to the song of death
Seeing the candles in the church next door
Now claiming their wicks have been before
To fight flames that crawl across each floor.

About The Whey They See

Taking our towns for silver and beads
Filling our minds and gardens with weeds
Blind to the power of rain and sun
Knowing not where their spirit will run.

On Chairs of English

Wicked the bantling
Who lives in these books
Compared to the schools
Of fish on their hooks.
Easy the knowledge
Slips out through our hand
Holding the poetry
On its head so to stand.

Power Byes

The lies you wear
Tear and treat delight.
Who wove them through
This evening burning bright,
Was it not the tongue of truth
That prades the scarlet letter?
Claiming all would see the day
When things had got much better,
Or was it just the sounding cane?
Tapping near to where
You had placed your feet.
As you did walk down Memory Land
With the poet who had lost his beat.

The Lady of Many Leaves

Props for the clever
Candles and cloth
Deep in her spell
The witch watches her broth
Unknowing the masses
Will soon drink from its foam
Then be off to the forest
To forever roam.

About the Future

Words can twist a fate
Duple time to time,
Still some grapes grow tart
While upon the vine.
The wicked marvel
Frequently
These days,
For they can see clear
Through the hulky haze.
Why the wisdom of
The most purest light,
Has come to emanate
These words this night.
Thus scapes the knowledge
To all baleful men
Unless they ask
The windward hand with pen.

Chef D'Oeuvre

A widow's curse of wicked words
Comes pouring out the ewer
Misunderstanding meets the night
From a long day on the shore
The tables set it will not fall
Its legs have most mighty knees
So place your order now! Before
The cook does what he please.

A Folio From The Wizard of Wameful

The lurching lurdanes need not step on forth,
For they line the walls with morbific force.
The ill heads of many will meet the cold mire
Before they begin to fathom out our fire.

The Kapellmeister Plays

Wager down good friend
Of the pursuit of knowledge,
Ye have been overcome,
Think not what might bring the magic,
For it has now begun.
To link the liquid serpents sail
Off to where no man's feet may run.
Or retell the clandestine tale
Which never claims that it is done.

Gropers of Darkness

Two graving docks were once provided
For the tailor of vestries to land
Freeing the bridges from their toll
While snapping chains at his command
He stepped through the empty ashpits
To wipe the work clean from his hand
Once the answer had slowly rose
Above his footprints in the sand.

Deceptive Knowledge

Footfalls on the waterfalls
We know where each man fell
Though what of the greatfalls
That not a man can tell.
Their secrets are our answer
And we never gave them doubt
Until we fathomed all
That said they were about.

No Belief In The Middle

Future present past
The seconds of the day
Are seen leaving fast
We want to hold them prey
Keep them from their end
Until we've found out how
Everyone of them
Pretends about the now.

The Husk and the Kernel

Midst the livelihood of peasants
Rough hewn their still feature spies
Finding friar books and seadrifts
Live inside of teachers lies
What's worth a few shillings
Will be sold as they meet
Not much for their spirit
And blistering of feet
Though a spark lights their twigs
Nigh by the foggy pond
That remarks with its flame
The lurking of each dawn
Where much less harsh a name
Is spoken out with scorn.

In His Flaming Verse

Fly in the eye of the hurricane
Then fall on the stairs of defeat,
Ye shall learn of the winds and their wrath
Leaving a taste not mentioned as sweet,
Which turns on the wings of the falcon
Then glides on the strength of the breeze
To land in the nest of knowing
Where spirits hide the field from the trees.

Beside the Mark

Closing the lid
Of the public's proud eye
Thieves take to the night
Towards the gold nearby
As chance would have it
They make off and guzzle away
Before deacons discover
Their gifts are gone far astray.

Fathom The Mischievous Folklore

A teaser at times with a tune that will twist
Like a hand through the fog all covered with mist.
A design of a dream drawn from our sleep
Inside of the secret dear Clotho will keep
Side of the fire where the willows weep in flame
Is coming a voice which gives each verse its name.

The Sly Test Thought

Knot the slight tease that poetry sees
Dropping from the roots of the minds
The barrel will fill to soon over spill
Moisture for the grapes on the vines
That are crushed to ply without the dregs
Keeping them safe in wooden kegs.

Knots That Know Their Capstans

Peer through the odd oracles
That this evening has found
And what they will tell about
As they slowly come around.
Sails in a full wind, a breeze in the air
Times and their talents, hidden will not share.
Why has the captain fallen from the stern
Without a care of floating
On the sea that has us learn?

Remove The Dust From Bookends

Remarkable personages of the times
March on the depths of thought
Regarding what rhymes
And has had their attention caught.
From old walls and towers they look
But cannot be simply freed
For the barghest and the bard
Have planted their every seed.

The Uneven Meet Her

An eluding invader well pronounced
To persuade her creator of,
The start, the bone, the heart,
Skull sides staring at the stillness
Say, "He decides our deep impressive part."

Knots For Us

The human mind is a sick breed, a poisoned flock
Unsure of when to go and more often when to stop.
Starved of its' own spirit
On its' knees neathe wisdoms whip.
A crew upon the seas, with no solid sailing ship.

Good Borning

Life has to be lived regardless of what people
may wish to do with it.
ENJOY
Not at any expense, although whenever possible.

WAR IS THE DISPOSING OF NEGATIVITY
UPON ONES' ENEMY.

PEACE IS THE POETIC POWER ENGRAVED
IN OUR SPIRIT.

The Republics Guarantee

Historically it's war in tea has exhumed itself,
From an acute accompaniment of astral beings.
Pretensious to the pendant of chemistry,
We clothe crowds in POETRY
Until those that have read,
See no carved customs frequent our style
Unless you wish to put the rimes on trial.

Bellcrank And Bellcanto,
Gear Up For The Old One Two

1. Colder than a canadian cookout
The words bounce off your page.
Your style and such it tags along
Behind the current age.

2. My thanks to you for such a compliment,
I chance more sweeter notes, have you once sent?
Crisp and crafty suit not I
And this discourse is sensed to ply.

1. What fits your foolish friendly mind
Has not one welcome to my kind
And if not a verbal vice of sorts
Might imply its best reports
Then latter may my voice invade
The world inside, you think you've made.

1. Sounds and counts with commanding quills
No poet ever gives me chills
And you've been first to call me down
To colder, lower, uncomplimentary ground.
If words said last are said at best
Then let these end like all the rest.

Brainwashed To Vote

"Dismantler of the future, navigator of the NOW
OUR TRIBE shows HOW!
The arrows of arrogance an avengening,
Find their feathers HERE. FLETCHING

Sleeping While Wide Awake

Words many times crumble at the feet of understanding
To evolve into monuments of knowledge.
Wisdom wins each game by being aloof
To description and the science of all meaning.
An adhearance to the more common sense of sorts will not apply.

Communist Plot

A walking forest fire, the dream avaitor lands,
Scouring the skull sides, attention avenues lead
From there light years from the fine roots of hair
The mind commands it has not a care.

You Don't Say

To compare is one of the most natural
And human traits shuffleing about
The abundance of astral activities.

CHAPTER TWO,
NO DISTINCT GEOGRAPHICAL ARTIFACTS

Upon The Keyboard

People as things are often best when left alone.
Including the subject and object,
A complete clause with two paws
Prowling around the room of understanding
Till wonder wilts about the wall
Extremes extract the glamour out of oneself
Fore the frets may find new notes.

She

If you stop and stumble over every clause,
The word itself will have you pause.

Scribed In The Log

This long shore with its spell
And a counch to hear well
The ocean and its roar
Has said neathe me
Lie men and their plea
Torn part from their core.
Once moved by the sword tip
Till no longer on ship
Creating the crew of unrest
Might their captain be asked
Or sure put to the task
To describe for them what is best?

CHAPTER THREE,
INCOGNITA MIND TERRA

Given The Pleasures

The lungs are first to know what's fair,
Deciding what's within the air.
The heart it's close to them it knows
Though only pounds it's fist on foes.
The truest song one ever sang
Was when the innocent were forced to hang.
Dangle within your mind this day
Above the earth where fools have say.
To know the sun and its first RAY
Is work so wild it's known as play.

BEN FRANKLIN SAID IF YOU WANT TO BE SOMETHING
AFTER YOU'RE DEAD AND GONE TO DUST, YOU
SHOULD WRITE SOMETHING WORTH READING OR DO
SOMETHING WORTH WRITING ABOUT.
LUCKY DOES NOT MEAN YOU ARE FORTUNATE = BLACK
ACE

Judging By The Cover

Over the air sounds come pound the image of space.
The first grade masters' approach Ieaves little to face.
A dozen wars without an end,
Claim peace was once their closest friend.
While lovers part and curse each stair,
They're forced to climb to be aware.
No poet ever feels the flow
It's something they are born to know,
Or first to find when they awake
To see each page with its mistake.

The Prolific Page Invader

Why so much must this one write
To pass and post before our sight?
If nothing ever read the same,
Would it increase this masters game?
Rime knows the glass on winters sill,
Where scenes of hills and mills stand still.
Fore shine and warmth decrease their pose,
Beneath the curtains' constant clothes.

SEGMENT TWO OF CHAPTER THREE,
VERBAL TELEPATHIC REPRODUCTIONS.

Inside

Time he writes around their view,
Beyond the most they ever knew.
Others fall short to never start,
With oils and brush the perfect art.
Framed and hung that day brand new,
Its nights begun to darken you.

The Pages Power

Never figure us out, we're always in.

At the Bar

We won the spilling bee.

All of Her Twisy

Set and savor this stew gone wild,
Hunters broth is our first gild

Too Lips

With no lust for more power,
We write and rain with sunlite shower.
The spring it waits to bounce and flower
Till it spires to see our tower.

Knots And Knots Of Rope

You answer too quickly.

Prey To The Land

The invisable reality from out of the claws set.

The Russian Windmill

In the house where grain is ground,
The great bell in the distance has no tongue to say it found.

Coined By His Own Poetic Meter

Bee there, no doubt,
I am first to serve and dish it out.
Your wings like things, have feathers worn
That cause most folks to curse and scorn.
For better not all doors they knock,
To find whom most has wound each clock,
Or while hands held them near to wall,
Still one decides what time to call.

Forest To Know

Workers of the pleasentrees, birds, lumberjacks, are falling leaves.

From Under the Staff

A shepherd and his dog
Rest the night away
While the flock it slowly moves
Through the meadow and its hay
The morning waits its own
Time and place to be
When no longer may the twain
Keep them from the land that's free.

Bellcrank Speaks, "Poe", lutes your bookstores.

AWETOMB

Over fact you ate, like the news, your shoes get old.
Over said and once foretold.
In these spires we weave our web
Until leaf life is sooner dead.

Cold Reality

Ice understands your top pick in the war tears.
Nerverawtic, a city person, unfamiliar with the woods;
'To hell with your spring, I've got a bed wrench.'

Bellcanto Spoke

As one becomes older,
Life more often presents its impossibility.
Life goes on and never finds itself.
Your arena of attitudes has not adapted
To accepting positive answers,
Nor possessing productive questions.
'Bellcrank'

To Capture Lies The Content

Painted matted
Left for further spoil
Next to spotted pottery
And it's few glimpse at toil
There stops and I
Too cleanse the stanzas lense
And scattered all the cameras bend on what pretends

Buy "Occam's Razor"

Whoa? Pen fore business beside the cold floor,
Feet had their mind, to first explore.
Overtakers of answers and written psalms knew,
When the words were placed tightly, then woven with you.
Ease hit the angle of each ivy league sot,
Till on the, "literatureship," their answer was caught.

Buy 'The Shadow He Cast'

Sense most you honestly make of things,
Unless their, diamond jewels or ruby rings.
Then small your mind, and near your sight,
For nothing is, from further right.
"A mix of worth and meanings core,
Tis not my mornings present chore."
When noon next strikes its twelfth-first hour,
You'll see who has the most of power.

Use your, youtensil

A bee of no hive am I, until they find their friend.
Now depth you say, is in being
Built high upon the page that has no end,
Still, I'll speak before you wish too
To take what I must first portend.

With No Burden of Beverage

When in a tussel, I'll tousle their kind
Yon, any tour of duty, their thoughts could once find.
Much more a teacher than a preacher,
My church gets no perch.
The bells from there pollute my air
And bases where I was born.
Eye dew not look nor write one book
That scholars call their own.
Inside this town, where we look around
Our library is our throne.
Critics' cry they cannot fly
Like birds who know their wings,
With nests of twig we will forever
Build the best of things!

CHAPTER FOUR,
GO BY THE BUY BULL

Alexandria

The server soon sleeps and crawls
Hoping none foresee the brawls
Before the town has become its own
Inside each barrel where shots are shown.

The Dis Covers

A hen on a hoot owl Mother Nature once saw,
When the poets designed and made up the law.
A flute for a favor
Came piping next door
When we woke from the flavor
Of having to explore.

May Sure Thing

We can take a dime or two
And toss it round the ranch.
We may make a leaf once new
Fall from its unsure branch.
Even though the wind once threw
Times two upon its tale,
The nature of the most common things
Began to have their scale,
They go away no wing.

Five Will Get You Ten

Pry or at least,
No question spins us round,
Less it's an answer without openness
To doubt on 1st ground.
Following atop
The once written page,
Meaning funds its stop
With the confrontation of its own age.
Who counts their joys and time
Inside each word,
Bound are books for some,
Where imperfect rimes are no longer heard.

Developing a New Cite

We've been bombed before and nearly could not move
From beneath the round table where our chips fell
Before they have our bets to most quickly prove.
Though takers take our wage with beer,
Has seen our eyes… when
On time to forget and take into the night
Gleaning more of their smooth shift an 1st surprise!
Passing the 5 knell exam
Bout as productive as a hen without a rooster.
More figures of speech than all the tongues
In the world
I know you've got a sure count on that
Hiding low inside your hat.

State Pig Pusher

We are not a weighted dress, waiting for our tip.
We are much more the sailing type, upon ever given ship.

SHIP

Our Captain calls the Sea's' his own,
When at night the crew's asleep
Upon any course a King could carve
And cause his Queen to weep.
Now, tears are full of salt they say,
Like oceans on this earth,
Though the hand with pen and mind so strong,
Made Moses what he's worth.
Table with its ten sure count
Like Shakespeare in a show,
Where plays are just for gays,
Who seem to surely know,
That rimes and frost and words work wild,
In dens of wolves worst fear
To face the dawn of each new day
Without another beer.

From Us!

With so many areas of endeavor
We may just once take this world
For its 1st ride, yond the ankled, chained,
Whom wish it's start to run an' hide.
Unfortunately, in most cases people are hiding themselves,
They are not pleased with their own presentation.

They are, One, During a Bout

Did I wreck your shun, coming from your mind?
Acceptance is not a quality for the common folks to find.
If magic was all I had, with tricks parked up my sleeve
I'd cast a spell all would learn and make their hearts believe.

Sic Pie Rats and Crumbs

I came from elfswhere,
The pen and page turn young there,
With old fruits crushed fresh
and aged to the finest wine.
Once words had men fall
Before they could quite once find
The meaning to themselves.

Pro Pester Rankle

Talent makes intelligence look like something
The cat dragged in while sitting at the show.
Next door the days grow deep in sin,
'Fore their roots may bloom below.
If natural were all word and phrase
There would be no idiots for me to raze.

On 2: Locations with Creativity

With all one's words boiled inside the ink
Not ever waiting for its ball to think
Or at least roll on across the line
Until the page itself can find
Meager men with their ego once wide
Who start to see and further ride
Into the sun or calmest shade
Where inside either two poems are made.

Poe! It's Gone

It's natural to have doubts,
You well-knitted fool
With your fitted counted shouts,
Heard outside of every rule
Till you come inside my constant written school
Where I drink and write my mind's worst fear
That stupidity shall not disappear.

A Joyful Turnabout

Greedyer than two goats just having knawed their trail threw hell,
He's back at the page for the wealthy to engage,
To leave their hearts free from the empty parts
That bring us all one good day to clearly say
Let's get us a poem a constant flow fast the past what at once was read
No originality may energize itself least they admit to having spead.
Then a balanced well-design with windmill's well tilt
Looking forward most fine upon all that we've built.

Concluding their Wants

Life here on traffic street never seems dull,
Always a whistle, a horn, a curious skull.
Find morguish the manor one has trolling in beat.
As if nothing occurs near in the midst of his feet.
Cloud walker,pedestrian on fire, no flames set
To the names for the marble city, sooner he wishes they would meet.

Congrats to the Addition

A new arrival to the family.
Yo! What a toy this certainly will be,
Admiring the strength brought upon our tree,
Seen topping the crux most significantly.

As We All Recall

May a pleague, a poison, pandemic sweep free,
The verse an all its well known potency,
Might the imagined, magic & merth
Fail stricken and fading from an ungreatful earth
Least on chances they gather to bet,
It's striking dominance may they never forget.

Life's Veil
Feeling sad for the folly that's fallen on you.

Searching out the permanent poetic ride,
Atop the wave twined high tide,
As she floats forgiving notes, and nicetee's,
She has our words weave through the breeze,
Rounds them off when pointy mad,
Cornering our smile to look less sad.
Previously purchased soul, spirit, body, mind
Living it out like it's all ours within
Shattering doubt & demise, venturing in all wars we will win.

Whispers wrally round the shrinkage.

Too rawtistic evil twins,
Unsure where their power stops, lesser to its begins.
Cast upon an unstable stage,
Deafened to the crowds growing rage,
Too soonly clean them from the page.
Leader's dream and also woe
On days the maze has less they know.
Blunt the fality reality hits cruel,
When twain and pain commence their fool.

Societies Motionless Movements

Bright was once and most care free
When futures were planned,
Continued to be no dramatic jumps
In cost toward all may be lost, to destiny.
Better the time seemed certain then to swell,
As more kindly the tales would wish us well.

Framed in the Thought Patterns

For the book for the please,
For the favor fallen stem upon its knees,
Near hung by the rime
And its adherence to time
Positioning points and the pronouns at best,
To pass and proceed any oncoming test.
Lighten the look and need to always inspect
that the allies may fear a chance of neglect.

Awkward the Market Where Many Seem to Feast

Buoyant & floaty the response comes today
Youthage steps forward with little less on display,
Floors to the stores franticly flip
Joined to the price of what's nice,
Stubborn it stands in ripe refussel too dip.

Woe for the Wit while Eating it Grins

More polish of style on looks
The cobbeler late for the opening to his superior trile.
Prosecutors dance bench bursting with guile,
Inhaling deeply the judge too is covered with smile.

Annomissly-Scattering

Flower arrangements for the fainted called fallen asleep,
Nicely now painted, hauls in the deep,
That nothing is made that forever may keep,
Pass on the dotted line,
Elsewhere will grasp the less known to be fine.

Names Fanning the Rat's Nest

Felt constantly sitting in the seat of control.
Not noticing ones whose banded about,
Strengthening the aim of an archer on the next floor,
Elevated to shoot shame as if never before,
Not shared as a well played game.
Let's leave it to rest, on its own, with its name.

Cuppeling the Obvious

The starter of each day & night
Voids the doubt the two shall fight,
Futures bound to come & say,
"Flood free, and share the value of this perfect play."

Composition Enjoyment

Let's fly past the heavens if such maybe done,
Or neath their magic memory & mirth.
The pope sings its the earthlings to near to my home,
May wellness come fast, to his being spirit & soul.
Off on the subject turning minds too ignore,
The sensitive passionate will finish that chore.
Fly free from the context as here there be none
And may not a word be written, if not for the fun.

Put in a Swinging Hunt Silhouette

Pages to plunder for the fields to full to fight,
With the darkness and setting of night.
A pattern, a potency gives forth its map,
Musical chairs to be first in its lap,
Words echo to where they may lead,
For sure & for certain as before it's from the land
known only for greed.

A Display of Political Illness

Shy they were banking on a victorious day,
Slumberly slacking, spreading their disdain,
Gossip & drool, upon their chosen prey,
They thought was a fool.
The rat's nest now scattered,
Lice licking their wounds objective in suit
Red tie & hat down to the whoof,
Sick silly & fat need we not any more proof.

Reference Toward the Missing

Well respected cut clean for pursuit
Never to let the day host for itself.
Beard broken, spoken 'neath soil,
Stands up and over the dounce dancing in delight,
Once here now we shall foil, the last of their spite.
Spitten and fitten, finer and free,
An adherence to substance twinning more now to their history.

Poetic Clockwork

What's to appear shaking the grounds
Sprouting signs may you never come near breaking the bounds
Bent on our back ghostly giving a mist to our mind,
Lands firmly in fact, there where true needs,
Need to share in good time.

Polishing the Curiosity

Mr. and Mrs. Settle with their son furtherguess
Arrived at the poets peak early to submit their composition
In search of the most comfortable position
Once the start and poems begin to multiply
Sad and glad came close to falling from each watcher's eye
A word smith sweeping beneath his bed caught by the maid
Holding the fairness of all good trade
Saying shall we let nothing be said and nothing be made?

Puppetized

Under the control of a mysterious puppeter
Given in too easily to made up mentions
Wearing a veil of good intentions
All clear coded near not to once they voted
To shut things down when efficient progress was best earned
By wishing to shut them up that they may share what they have
learned.

The Wandering of the Adventurous

A vacancy of vagabonds gypsis rare seen in their delight
Days of vagueness voice to beg less
As disappearance makes more the mind to spin
All round the evil make up as faces loss their grin
Losses deep in wonder when was their time to win.

What the Public Square Recalls

From a land that turned to third
Where little thoughts were seldom heard
There grows the physical mounting mess
Where minds in masses come to confess

Anne Marie and Forever

Anne Marie I miss you so
More than ever could you know
This time apart is hard for me
It's only you I wish to see
Had I ever known that now
Would be like this be wondering how
Long before I may hold you tight
And be together again each night
These words are small unlike my love
For you that flies more high above
Anything or one who'd say
I love is small and will pass a way
It's just be you I live this life
And thank all things that you're my wife.

DOPEN = Living life under the influence of either this, that or the other.

FATHOMINITY = The ability to perceive beyond. The potentials of knowledge and wisdom.

VOWVOIDANCE = The absence in mind of creative thought.

HECTIVITY = A fever created in the nineteen nineties within the minds of humanity for the need of nature.

ATTILATIC = A removal of all designs and foreshadowing of ignorance appearing in the path of learning refinement.

PLYSPECTRUMSPEER = The gleaning of certain new realities that are inevitable with practice of sorcery.

DESIRENETIC CODE = The origin of the compulsion for material wealth.

MIRRORTIVITY = Deep in reflective thought.

SPICELINAGE = Tasteful word usage.

CULTGARDENEER = A caster of the growing spell.

READISTISITY = A quality of mind that enables one to see multiple meanings in one written line.

LIGHTMARTUITION = An ability to land in unresearched areas of the mind.

FOLIOSCOPTIC = A poetic page of a sorcerer.

PRADE = The praenominal art involved with the meaning of the word.

ONDRAGY = Astral energy fields.

OVRING = Superior astral sorcery.

TOEFEVORATION = Tear of an invisible enemy.

FLOWLINATIC = One who writes with excessive rhythm.

SKYSENTRICK = To believe in the above.

ARMNATION = A large group of fools that still believe a physical war may still be won.

BIDMORDEATH = Concluding that the more life is created, the more it will dissolve.

FOLIOFEVER = An obsession with reading or writing books.

KNOTLY, = An opposing thought process.

ROLEAN = Brainfood

CLIPSEW = An island rhythm, a melody breeze, the above formular.

OBTRUCITY = The unknown! Invaders of the common knowledge, whom build it beyond its everyday humdrum. Heavy though not dull.

RICHENTARY = Evolutionized vocabulary = Words worth a moment of consideration.

PUZZELEST = A designer of thought.
               Contradistictive of idioelectric uniform.

DAYMENTED = Events and activities angled away from the NIGHT hours. An adjective.

RAYSPOND = The reaction of living organism to sunlite.

LIFTUOUS = Purely focused on intellectual and artistic endeavors.

COMMONILITIES = Average, everyday humdrum, mindsets.

OUTRESTED = Not amused, nor interested.

TWISY = In Love.

TRICKULATED = Disguised by one's own imagination.
Bitterly crafty, your first taste has begun.

DEAD = Nothing, nor no-one to make wonder.

AWEBIT = Ones ability to make wonder.

WINCHEREYES = Protection from cold stupidity, an elevated literature course applied to one's life.

FEDINFESTED = Beyond money, beyond being toppled a U.S. Citizen.

ANIMALMENTARIAN = One into animal rights excessively.

TOEBEER = A condition of the mind controlled by poetry.

SILVERNEARS = Antediluvian knowledge.

GELUS = Lack of respect for artful words.

ONNEST = Propper feathers upon one's roost.

CARETCHER = A personality that easily embraces art, and literature.

GELICA = Accustomed to our approach.

COREWRECK = One's soul, spirit and mind.
Designed in a more unique fashion.

SHOETHINGTHABREEZE = Talking.
One often has to watch what they say and more often how they say it.
Distraught with life, beyond compare, everyone has to once despair.
The tallest man on hills of ants to imperfect rhymes told by chants.

MYGRAYTHING = People who move domestically, with environment being their main issue.

VIETWOMEN = A necessary element for food thought, the main operative for cognizance.

THEURGY = Never near the realm, nor upon the helm of understanding.

PARTEASE = An element of enjoyment, exposed by a higher command with the power to control one and all's conversation.

QUARTERFARCATION = The ability to speak loudly and not say a word. Time heals their wishes.

DESTORIED = Readers of poetic value, open to new understandings.

MOTORVEILSHUN = A commander at birth.

FLITCHER = A filtering bird for the moldy minds nest.

AMLITION = Poetic motivation.

SKULBEAMIC = Weighing out the ordinary.

PAPATEATOES = Those most commonly controlled by a string, those who find comfort in flocks of the ordinary.

BEEAH = A brew, till point of view.

BARYEITY = One with many watering holes.

ARROWGANT = Loss of control with one's ego.

BOUGHTENEST = One who pays money for a bird.

PROMOATED = One's home is one's castle.
Bellcanto Speaks, "Jest buy for the party when it's crashed."

OUTERBILITY = An astute astral talent.

SEXSEED = An accomplishment with no virus.

BOWQUETION = Once upon an event.

BARNFULL = One's personal library.

TOETOW = A concise view, a bit more than clear.

FALLOWING = Top of the page.

WINNING = Throwing the towel out.

BEEFORE = The sting of futuristic literature with antedoluvian attributes.
Some people work hard all their lives trying to be themselves and never get the job done.

VOCABLOCK = Unable to describe clearly, with no presence of articulation.

A RICHYARDTATOR – An autocrat of the future.

FEEBILLISTIC = Life lived yond the ace of excellence.
                    Unmanicured maturity.

VOIDOMATIC = An ability to induce wonder.